MY *Scarlet* WAYS

Tanya Larkin

winner of the 2011 Saturnalia Books Poetry Prize

saturnalia books

Distributed by University Press of New England
Hanover and London

Saturnalia Books
105 Woodside Rd.
Ardmore, PA 19003
info@saturnaliabooks.com

ISBN: 978-0-9833686-3-2
Library of Congress Control Number: 2011945979

Book Design by Saturnalia Books
Printing by The Prolific Group, Canada

Cover Art: Isa Brito
Photo credit: Amber Marsch

Distributed by:
University Press of New England
1 Court Street
Lebanon, NH 03766
800-421-1561

Grateful acknowledgement is made to the following publications in which these poems have appeared, sometimes in different form than they appear in the book: *Boog City*: "Fog Machine"; *Conduit*: "Baby Epic"; *Electronic Poetry Review*: "Hookey," "Queenright," "Diana of the Selves," "Market Day"; *Free Radicals: American Poets Before Their First Books*: "Cho-fu-Sa," "With Cheerful Speed"; *Hanging Loose*: "Essay on Style (II)," "Transport," "Skaz"; *The Hat*: "Plum Gig," "Heaven and Hell Are Real Places," "Blue Nurse Movie," "Serenissima," "Town"; *Isn't It Romantic: 100 Love Poems by Younger American Poets*: "Cho-Fu-Sa"; *Ploughshares*: "Consort"; *Satellite Telephone*: "Prospects," "Elegy"; *Quarterly West*: "Winding Sheet," "Mare Clausum"; *Xantippe*: "Market Day"; *Zoland Poetry Anthology*: "Argument," "Enemy Love Song," "In the Mountains, There You Feel Free."

Thank you to my family and friends. For guidance and support, thank you to Peter Richards, Joanna Hershon, David Blair, Suzanne Buffam, Eric Bennett, Derek Buckner, Joanna Fuhrman, Amy Lingafelter, Gillian Kiley, Benjamin Paloff, Cody Petterson, D.A. Powell, Srikanth Reddy, Spencer Short, Sam White, and Sam Witt.

for my sisters, Karen and Katie

To put this World down, like a Bundle –
And walk steady, away,
Requires Energy – possibly Agony –
'Tis the Scarlet way
                              —Emily Dickinson

TABLE OF CONTENTS

I.

Transport	1
Acqua Alta	3
Serenissima	4
Real Pastoral	6
Petulance	7
Enemy Love Song	8
The Heavenly Bodies Are Bowls of Fire	9
Town	11
Foundling Wheel	12
Blame it on Rilke	13
Elegy	14
Arson	16
Argument	17

II.

Essay on Style	21
Skaz	22
Fog Machine	23
Direction	24
Kite Everlasting	25
Consort	27
The Headdress	28
Plum Gig	29

Diana of the Selves 30

Market Day 31

Aubade 32

Hookey 33

Heaven and Hell Are Real Places 35

Baby Epic 36

Bluestocking 37

Essay on Style 39

III.

In the Mountains, There You Feel Free 43

Queenright 44

Blue Nurse Movie 45

Middle Distance 46

Intelligence by Far 47

Inheritance 49

With Cheerful Speed 51

Prospects 53

Winding Sheet 54

Mare Clausum 56

Cho-Fu-Sa 59

*** Years Old 61

Coda 62

Notes 65

I.

TRANSPORT

To feel finally used up by the beauty
of the world, truly milked, as if I'd just
given suck to a brood of hungry stars. To be
for several moments nature's one and only
wet nurse, all matter depending
·on the speed at which I flow, the speed
at which I flow accruing voices hydro-
muscular and braiding through the soil
a proletariat anthem that sweetens wells
cranks swings and lands kids on their feet.

The voices flush out debris
the broken faces galloped through.
One says, pull the satins from my mouth.
Fleets and fleets of throbbing ships
crowd my milk with eager sails
saluting terra incognita, or wherever
the voices go, whatever they say
if it happens, I shall, if they stop, I will
if they fail, I will faint and resurrect
like a circus tent at dawn
first in one town, then another.

In one of these towns, a coiled
snake, snug and sleeping
in the rings of a rubber hose.

I was this pink, sun-cradled snake.
I grew anarchic red. I was a mother
who buried her love so deep
even death couldn't find it.
So gone into things, resigned
to winds, charmed by use—
they strapped me to a prow for luck.

Acqua Alta

Sisters, don't let sisters
ride the chandelier.
It's just a Turkish tea set
with a drunk seductive chime
like the bell in the broken doll's head
we loved to kick around.

It won't swing you
as far as the window
or above the mute canal
mossed over with thoughts
neighbors keep to themselves
about sorrow's relation to glamour,
the American way.

It's not so bad
the sound of losing at love.
When we broke off the arms of the statue
she softly came alive.

SERENISSIMA

When lonely, I lie down in my hair
and say, gondola, gondola. I lie down

in my hair and displace God,
who before I arrived—insolubly sad

and dragging a lagoon—was everywhere
singing the unsayable, playing us

like flutes and finding all the stops,
the diary stop, the brain-kiss stop,

the cruel-milk-falling-from-the-eaves
stop. Once I broke a friend's diary

open, smashing the lock against a rock.
I too had my stops and was played

played thoroughly until lying down
like twilight's grenade or an egg

twilight lays every five thousand
years, I measure the proportion of God

to self. There is precisely this much me
in the room. And I know precisely

because I am not that girl off to powder-
puff in the leaves thinking, love

come smother me faster. I am
a paperback soaking in rain,

o to be read by rain, the rain turning
your pages with its fat greasy finger

or the gutter in which it comes rushing:
an axe behind glass, no emergency, no—

a tower, an otter, a spindle, a drum,
or thrush, the bird and the disease,

all of history would do, or just
a sandwich, a lech, a semi, an alp

but the old world I am not. The new world
flies out and never comes back.

REAL PASTORAL

How good it must feel to play through the girls,
thinks the dew, the corn, the well-informed blimps
but especially the handkerchief of dew in my skirt
as I play through the girls leaving divots in vulgar
touch-me-not shapes. Goodbye, girls, I'll see you
later in the place where your wings are trussed
and my limbs serve the devouring green.
I have a natural stroke that frees maidens first
whose jeans are riding up. Then I get to you
because it's only in the swing that one remembers
how showering at night makes me one of those girls
who can batter a kiss into a ship, the ship into a fort
as I reach what I deem the most foreign soil.

PETULANCE

Landlock—where God stands
in for water, I nurse a thirst
that equals belief. Spoiled
brat of the earth, I am
scavenging for hidden
gifts in every wind-hatched
field. First I was a Jesuit
then a glass-blown town.
Now I am ripping off Advent
days before they arrive. Arrive!
This little scene is not good
enough, nor is this donkey—
knocking sleep off the shelf.

ENEMY LOVE SONG

You are a beautiful tense with no language to live in.
A mean pathological slit-show with no stuff to disperse
or mirror to break into flower when I put words
in your mouth like—this harness itches
these breasts leak half-deciphered speech.
I unchain the animals and place them sleeping
around you. I saw you there soaking in grass until grass
felt its sex and I shouted, smite me like a nation
It is you, who washes death's small posable head
with soft licks. One day you will lick it entirely away
for it is tasty, licking an entire salt woman,
advancing world peace. I brush against your face
and sworn enemies explode

THE HEAVENLY BODIES ARE BOWLS OF FIRE

Who cheats at spin the bottle to tell
more truth is who dies to play

me now. This is the Spinster Show;
steer me to the closet and cowl me

there. I object to everything
you have ever said or wanted:

the hip glance, the mitred breath,
objectivity. . .the dead heat of

our small, unconverging lives.
There are two rules. One woman

ignites and goes out in equal
measures. The other wants to be

razed periodically, like a world.
There is nothing left to ask

with—my body, last of my kin
and kindling. Orphelin/orpheline,

grow into my fist and open it.
This bowl of fire doesn't speak.

This spinster has merely to spin
to housekeep too thoroughly

and lose whole days on one piece
of furniture. I'm reported missing

at the mirror when I think of you,
you suckhole of sincerity, you

glistening knob fallen from
the door. The sky is dusking down;

I am dizzied, am living in the exact-
ing fold of an ecumenical blind-

fold, entirely hidden from God,
the sky on its knees. I feel to see, I see

out with a rusting tack to prick
stars that have been pricked

before. I'd be entirely hidden,
screened out of vision,

but for that phosphor crumb
on my mouth he will not wipe away.

TOWN

The world outside my window is a mirror I can't break.
I make a face at my neighbor and she makes a face back.
Our hellos lock letters and fly to hell where they copulate
and cry because they can't have kids.

This is a city where no one meets by chance. No one lies
about her past or pretends anything she's not
by stitching a flower to her crotch or saying, I was sired by the wind!
I have no mother, no father. My ancestors—only vowels.

My double does not flirt with me or menace me by dying
slower than I do. My double does not exist.
That is the kind of city this is. It's lost all its teeth.
Sometimes I taunt it. I say, take a bite of me, go ahead.
Sometimes I feed it breadcrumbs soaked in broth.

Foundling Wheel

Since no one remembers my birth I must part myself
like a curtain and walk through it again and again as long as it takes
to accept I am my own big baby and for that acceptance
I must thank the relentless applause however silent
the empty seats like sockets with no eyes. I was not conceived
in the dark theater the dark theater
conceived me. I orphaned myself deep
in the bowels of my heart where I drank to my arrival
a wine pressed from my major and minor cries.
There in the courtyard with just a few things to swing on
and the images I summoned as I swung all the images
that raised me like a battery of nuns—so many open black wings—
I fed myself and was proud I dressed myself and was proud but never
so much as when I stripped myself down to nothing but a tune.
An anisette breeze scrubbed the air and led away from my heart.
A mother image whispered in my ear,
o hothouse orphan we nearly grew from seed,
your sweet suckling mouth was always astray of the source.
Assume your proportions and make mamma proud.

BLAME IT ON RILKE

Now is a scandal, a mouth burning down and still trying to speak.
Ten thousand mothers are running toward it.
They want to plant it with a firm kiss
to save it or snuff out the danger—or simply
shut it up.

Elegy

You lived such a perfect life that when you died your life
became mine I knew it when the sun struck my face
for a moment I did not need to say where are you
crouching between two notes you never heard while alive
or on a pile of rope sniffing out sex-past or sex-future
forgetting your mother and father the color of milk
there goes love's hierarchy a pleasure only felt
by pleasure seekers not the pit of a fruit eaten all at once
and thrown into space I say your name here please
tell me what it is like to be eaten all at once
then punish me appropriately send me blows from afar
or answer like a god with silence and weather
nods of coincidence or all of literature I promise to listen
because I remember the moment you left your life
to me I was under the coats pretending to be a coat
finding your smell then losing it before I had the chance
to find your coat put it on so you could never leave
there were so many coats if only you knew how many
you would take the number between your teeth and stick it
with your sharpest because it is the job of the dead
to destroy numbers each and every one of you with the bodies
you no longer have carnivorous songs you took to your grave
I cannot do it alone signing all of your names to my letters
saying aren't I brave dear so and so having feelings at all
having feelings and smashing them to bits with these very words
is that what you are doing you say from your several

hiding places stitched into the thighs of those who are famous
among the dead and never among the living hanging happy
in a sack full of ashes on market day in the intelligent toy
my child refuses to play with no that is not what I am doing
then what are you doing saying my name and moving these words
what are you doing what am I doing—making some room

ARSON

I misread the word arson for person.
That is how it started. I could see
through the words to the words
they might have been had they stuck
to their diet of colors and fumes.
Had they never grown up
in such a broken home as this
where out of fear we sleep in the same bed
dreaming the same dream of melting
our mother down for scrap.

She has practically offered. Besides,
it is wartime, we are childless, we do not
want her to outlive our usefulness.
These days I cannot get high enough
to vandalize the moon. I cannot get low
enough to eat earth and like it.

ARGUMENT

None, none, my dear, none none,
is a song we sing ourselves to sleep,
sleep itself a leaky refrain, a hand
that skims the wheat before plot intrudes,
a lukewarm heiress, a marriage annulled
to elope with a color, sovereign as a beast.
Once difference made me bold
but now it is sameness. A good poem
shoots me like trash into space
and the rags I call mother fall into the sea.

ESSAY ON STYLE

I care about style but it's not everything.
It's only anything insofar as I need it
to survive the sad pulp of late afternoon,
the sublime languors of a loved one as he or she
decides to have me or not. Therein lies the paradox
of style staining the couch with sweaty dreams,
of being something more than a misty crossroads
where one waits to be assumed or absorbed
by the ether, by a higher truth in the margin,
the blacked out fields where desire is still
wanting to die. But in the crossroads you keep it
alive, drinking a flight at the shrine, stealing days-
old offerings, splayed fruit and silk flowers.
You wear it all to become more mysterious,
to dress the senile trees in kitschy lights.

SKAZ

As if the juice could be brighter
and the pudding be still.
As if surging through a villa
vatic in a corset o where is the cordless
the lost disc of postpunk seraphim rending the skies.
As if to rip the lining as if to kiss the hem
and stones tumbled out stones carried so long
that as they struck the ground became jewels.
As if a dance floor shattered.
As if slung low in a cab the neon smear erasing the number
I was trying hard to remember.
As if it weren't so cold I had to write non-stop to keep warm.
As if from his shoulder you couldn't see
a rope bridge strangled and twisting in rushes.
As if in exile my hand at the candle.
As if one foot in the door of the doom room.
As if the grass didn't bleed when you walked on it.
As if Satan didn't look so cute when defeated
his oversized wings curving over his head.
As if the message weren't written in invisible ink.
As if seasons didn't matter but it's your blankety blank life
Southern California or lack thereof.
As if Nebraska said give me a hill so I can jump.
As if for sooth we went pretending in feathered masks.
As if a little penance and a lot of espresso.
As if the password weren't *password*.
As if she said when he asked again if there was ever a chance.

FOG MACHINE

Since every note cannot be
a dying one I throw down the key
in a sock and sing all the way up
the bridge is black it grows
from my chest raging fate and health
as it breaches toward the future
then demurs like breath to find you
always on your way a chance of rain
in your step and wolves in your sack
tossed high on a bounce and falling
on your shoulders with a soft melodic
thud that sets your blood to bark
How now young smell The traffic
combs through while you stand still
sucking the salt from a scab
though the sign says walk

Direction

God is a stupid word but I'm going to
use it anyway: a blue foot was crushing my lungs.
In the shallows of my breath, small animals
were drowning as we're all drowning in God.
What could I do to save them, pinned as I was
mouth-to-mouth was no option there was no
choice but accept the foot into my chest, let it
kick in my ribs with its all-seeing heel, mash my
heart into a perfumed nectar too sweet for none.
Who am I and what's this pain to get in the way
of a deep deliberate step? None of my business
where it's going or if it's just getting lost.

KITE EVERLASTING

Against gravity, you tried me.
You tried me against all manner
of skies, and I tried too. Bowing my forehead
to the ground before I caught a thermal
and shook the latin from my sides.

Against a gust, I thrust
the hard cross of my flat chest
and strained the wind for music.
I dove for something remotely tonal.
I grubbed for more sky and did the work
of hanging plumb like a fact
when the string began to slacken.
No drowsing at its end. No fleeing
from my owner's hand
without the anticipation
of being reeled back in.

One day the blue-black ravens dispersed
as I strove to be one of them—your fault, your hand
and the tenuous string that made me think
I was alive. I was nearly shamed into sleep
and drifting toward the branches: staged math,
a shoe tarred and feathered in honey and leaves,
a tooth you lost and forgot to cash in,

not a kite any more but a thing to help you
dream that each color die of internal hemorrhage,
that you save the pariah moan. That you alone
with your even breath and calloused fingers
have been chosen to pick the burrs
from a crying child's hair.

Or was it lightning that did it? That time
you refused to go home, both of us on fire.
Through me you found what?
A way to avoid team sports?
The illusion of flight?
A little electricity?

CONSORT

I am the disease that confirms
evening is normal and desirable.
Evening, which behaves
like an odor or taboo
then crushes a hillside into its breast,
and all the hillside's murmuring towers,
the ten grazing horses locked to its base.
Who isn't bullied now and then by the soft
slurry dialect of stars which are lodged
in the sky and my side?
In the sky, orphaned kites never smell
gender or kiss any mouth that swallows
me whole. I let go of each kite,
resenting my hand.

THE HEADDRESS

All the breathing in the basilica
pushes a headdress out to sea
where it sails out of earshot
past you and I so thoroughly
distracted by the crease in my accent
the oiled skiff that embarks
from your glance we think perhaps
we made the headdress from looks
thrown across a party and longbows
shot backwards through the years

A child makes a headdress from various
things a horse of its own brooding
fidgets from the bath but mostly spit
and the dream of being sucked free
of her flesh and filled entirely with milk
she crowns the water where the floor falls
sheer beneath her the headdress humming
to be carried out with words the dream
the brightening pain that thinking makes so

PLUM GIG

Happiness is unanimous the sun
bites down with its one blunt tooth
and cracks the glaze of all the sleeping
animals I am one of them and so are you
and you and you who lash me with your smile
once my dream has ended I like the day
to smart like a wound that tightens
around me as it heals I want to say, sky!
I would keep you open all night even if it hurt
because happiness is dangerous it lets down
my guard so a wolf-torn wolf and secondhand
chiffon come to cuddle inside me and angels
binge on human food so many children
from countries I've never even heard of
ask each other inside me, do you wanna run?
but too many women and men have come
to glimpse Jesus Christ inside me and he has not
shown up some think he has stood them up
they lie down together inside me others keep
waiting until Jesus shows up and cries
all over they go home satisfied and wet

DIANA OF THE SELVES

Once we used prayer to build up the body
and fatten it through the night. Dirt
was the trophy against the ankle hollow
or crammed into the knuckle crease—
the distance we had traveled to a more
dizzying height. There the wind keened
out of hunger and put its snout to the road.
We looked back and saw our younger
selves trying to keep up, whipped almost
to transparency. But I was quickest
to my quiver. My arrow was out.
I learn more from missing—when I miss.

MARKET DAY

I want to make a terrible noise inside you
worse than tourniquets and scalded pigs
in maiden weather dress a super-smart
flesh and blood oracle-smelling noise
where the dead can argue back
and finger you out of your fingering hole
and punish your sequin with real flayed light
for I too can go to market with my brothers
I am a child of forward parts forgetting
the radical skill message of my hands

AUBADE

This is my day, says the light,
go forth and break yourself against it
because you have become nothing

but yourself, occasionally a window
with a view or a single leaf carousing
through the air but certainly not
the cheek it catches and claws with affection

three whole seconds of true leaf affection
you missed because you were off with your blankey
your nose in the moss a finger in the lining.

HOOKEY

Put me out, put me out. I fevered my way
out of school again. Then forgot to leave the lie:

the play at palsy, my best friend, mercury and
a crown of sighs. I was burnt tongue, grump girl,

doped up on my souring skin, nursed napward
by colorless, toxic seconds. My dream was brief;

it briefed me. The book I was reading bit me,
and I tried to bite it back, but left the dream

for another, jawing at the air. There I loved
my name as if it were not my own, as if

all the Tanya's lived in a Tanya-forest without
bodies—I could smell them burning

supper. Now all my flesh is glass and all life
just a picnic of reflection: there's flame and then

there's flame, turning itself inside out for you.
Sleight of mouth, a blue door

in the flame's middle, the white-hot knob,
an idle girl's tabernacle. Ah, exile, how easy

it is to fall for myself, to erect and
embroider my body. I am a flower

and a condition. A supine sniper in bed,
myopic—picking off the swan in the corner

(twilight's muscle) a bullet through its neck.
How else should I measure my leisure?

HEAVEN AND HELL ARE REAL PLACES

Goody for them but I'll keep walking
trailing my dew my opalescent happiness
goo over the rooftops and chamomile fuzz
through the swan-choked pond a tiny
cathedral hidden in the ferns really swinging
with stained light a pink that keeps peeling
itself paler and virgin blue darkening into
more-experienced blue I had to shrink
my ego to enter by sucking on a candy
fiercely until it disappeared it was that easy
you simply have to stop thinking and use
your tongue somehow then you can fit
into the most coveted hiding place be it
tender or spiked or sashed with moans
like the itty-bitty altars in this toy cathedral
where I thank God for giving me autumn
and unwrapping it so violently shaking
the knife in the air nicking the light then
hacking it in two and mincing it to bits
and my happiness in this infinitely dying
light what would I do if I couldn't release
a little liquid now and then I would die
of happiness for sure I would burst

BABY EPIC

Gird your mysterious loins, I am trying to think
of a pick-up line beginning with war and ending with peace.
Inside it, horses will foam at the mouth. A row of archers
shall go down on one knee. Dear, my heart
shall be strung so tightly that when a bell tree shakes its locks
and sparks the thought of me inside you, pitching tents,
a happy marauder bound for the interior, teaching natives
my traditional songs as I slash and burn a path
to a darkness you never knew but hoped I might find, I will
let my crutches fall and charge into your searing affection
pretending to be healthy, a real sport with a grass-stained
smile, a bouquet of anguishes forever at my back or tossed
into a blood-fed stream coursing half-dissolved cries.
There you and your ages stop to water at my pulse.
There my eyes roll back and my gaze treads the air
for as long as it takes to tie an unbreakable horse to my stare
that inconsolable horse your loneliest age, a rank buckskin
annoyed by breath and only calmed by an enemy's dying look.
In my fist you put the reins to your ages, some slack
and some taut, dragging me away to inaudible strains.
Under burning confetti they drag me
and I can almost hear what they hear.

BLUESTOCKING

Because you carry at all times an idea of beauty,
and because your rage for order wants everything
in its place, you stick me with a look that begrudges me
my swagger, my drift, my face exhausting petals, old crony of the sun,
which owes me cash-money though I could care less if I ever get paid.
Hence my swagger, which you think a refusal to live
inside of anything, a will to put the wreck back in recreation,
flood the annual flower show clear to the top until the crooked pavilion,
master cut like a gem with a lunatic shine, springs a delicate fracture
that shoots ever-branching through the glass until the pavilion pops,
a bloom itself that releases fragrant steam, Pah Pah, into the sky,
setting the ladies free to float in underskirts and culottes,
clutching black ferns, black roses in their teeth
as they bob through the burbs, expressing like me
a dangerous desire not to be contained
but to stream out on the grace of a current
cold as it may be, my face ransacked by a forward breeze
that rains petals to the gutter, souvenirs
to press between the pages of your monstrous guide.
Under me let it say, proud to be flora and fauna though hard to identify,
my swagger mistaken for everything but nothing
so simple as a dance. I throw out a shoulder thinking up music,
like not even spring can deny me spring in my chops
when armed with the knowledge
that only the body can break from the body,
being all that we've got to work with.
It's not that I refuse to live inside of anything,

just my God's much farther than yours—
not a quick scramble up the light.

ESSAY ON STYLE

What are you style? Besides something to fool
around with until the real thing comes along
a way to say, here I interject a little weather. I click
through so-and-so's vapors on apocalyptic heels.
When I write fiction, I call you the distance
between me and my characters. In a poem, are you
the distance between me and myself? Is the goal
not to have you at all but to burn in my own flame
not just sit there by the fire singing songs and
warming my hands? That seems a little extreme,
even boring in the way suicide and adultery
are boring—though we gasp and fall to the floor.
More likely, style, you're an instinct for self-
preservation, so I don't blame those who hide
in you. Occasionally they must spring forth
for a breath of fresh air or a hot meal. Then I am
there for them as I am here for myself now, praising
the distance between us since without distance
there's no love—no room to cast oneself out.

IN THE MOUNTAINS, THERE YOU FEEL FREE

Here kissing lasts a country mile.
Here idiot blooms and tenderness raked.
Somewhere in the sun we have lost
our way and settled inside a gilded maw.
Virgins and tykes grip the clover for ballast.
Crones doubled-over speak to their sores.

Together we go lordless on a breeze
like bells on the loose which all of a sudden
soften the silence with ghostly peals.
I run my silver down your parts.
You run your silver down mine.

What vessels we are, what sad lace maps.
I hustle my tears for a view from your eyes.
The peak of every color shouting each to each.
The sun has a body to go with its head.

QUEENRIGHT

She ripped the hive from the hollow
coming unhinged like the hive.
Brained it, broke it open on a tree
that had fallen across her lap.
Her hair dripping toward us, each lock
skinned by noonlight, ropy and blue.
Feeding in the darkness of her hair
she tastes the different-colored honey
ringing the brood—

redbud, serviceberry, cherry and plum.
Then the honeycomb tore, she tore it
and dumped the brood
into her mouth—
voiceless, wingless, their appetite,
calling her by scent.

She seemed to eat not for hunger
or pleasure but because she wanted
to be alone, uncomplicated
like wind.

Blue Nurse Movie

My little dark one, my little death,
she said, nothing exists until you lick it.
I said I wanted to be licked.
Portrait of Her Laugh Portrait
of Her Laugh. Two horses came
to the city that night, nuzzled
the shutters open. They neighed
flashing their teeth in her sleep,
eating the Portrait of her Laugh
as they painted it, she laughed herself
awake, a wrecking ball with too much
eyeliner. She made me wear her jeans
with heels. On the dance floor she said,
I like it. My jeans were too small
but she wore them anyway saying
my ass looks great in your jeans.
Look at the cypress, I said, it really
knows how to use its drama. Lick it,
she said. But it already exists, I said.
This time my nurse didn't laugh. No
more portraits I guessed when she said
every day she pulls out patients' catheters
and wipes the shit off sheets, rolling
those sheets out from under them, you
can smell it a mile away, their singular
death as it travels, she travels with it
keeping both of us company.

MIDDLE DISTANCE

The painter is half-blind and paints without her glasses on.
The landscape is either furred or pearled depending on the light.
The landscape is closer to being itself because she can only see half of it.
The rest is faith and lets the landscape alone.
Half-alone, one might say, is the optimal condition—
but not for a landscape which yearns to be either full or emptied of gaze.
Half-alone, a branch snaps, and the orchard begins to hemorrhage.
Half-alone, it resorts to speech. It brands the car-sick daytrippers
with epiphanic stuff. If love is the answer to death, what is
the answer to love? says a boy to his kite.

When she doesn't wear her glasses, the painter feels hunted
that she is getting in the way of something that is watching
and something being watched, i.e., the landscape, which
if she weren't there, could fully be itself and eat the air in peace,
not leaving a crumb. Now and then it looks up with sorrow from its meal.
If I were blind, she thinks, it would never be distracted. On the other hand,
if I could see perfectly, it would starve in exile waiting for permission.
Thank heaven, I am at least half-blind and thus half seen through.
The sense of being hunted is bunk, divine bunk.
If I only I were stupid and happy and had 20/20 vision
I would paint the invisible without remorse or the effort
that comes with remorse, she thinks. I would gladly be the first to be fanged
by either animal. For frantic sunshine spoken through a back.
For a ventilated grief, a stop-motion collapse.

INTELLIGENCE BY FAR

It begins and ends with a woman
hanging from her mouth,
harnessed to the sky
by a sleek steel braid
that goes up and up
into the bottomless dark,
a place where stars are painted on
and weather gives lessons
on indifference and sleep.
The cruel arches of her feet.
Her bodice a glittering crust,
a stiff brocade inflicting sparks
that blur into a ring,
an icy planetary ring,
as she spins into a coil
that ravels her away.
A solemn whir hushes the crowd
as she jets toward the ground
about to screw into the sand
when she springs back up
wheeling tight against the sky.
This is the moment the winding slows.
We see her age, the Lord's strength in her jaw.
The cable groans in her mouth
with human complaint.
It has a past, it has desire.

It was something she said
she wants to take back.

INHERITANCE

Today I strive but tomorrow I will go
at the pace of an heir. No need to hurry
through anything, even sadness or cold,
since time is money and tomorrow I shall have
plenty of that. It is my turn now as I take long walks
friend of the master and his hound, its bark
as it joins the dawn bells, so fresh from a good
night's sleep they would break and gallop west
out of their holy stalls singing, God cannot
get you out of time only money which shall give
both sides of the coin. Heads mine, tails mine.
Mine, the whole body of the coin as I sink
into a bath, a glossy penny or filthy quarter
tossed into a fountain by a child in knee socks.
There, underwater, I hold my breath and think
hard about her wish and hard about my breath,
that baton handed off, the torch I was asked
to run with. There was much urgency, much end,
then when I needed breath but now I reject
anything I can have easily, which is quite a lot
now that I am rich. Just think of all the stuff!
The coastal property, the vertiginous erudition,
a wizened pine to give advice when you lean
long against it, reading a book which sheds gold
dust as you turn the pages, staining your fingertips
so that everywhere you touch, a knob, a cheek, a fork—

you leave a mark that says, I am wise, or rather
I own an antique book and every marked and
unmarked tree in this double silent old growth
forest belongs to me. All the past belongs to me.
Or it could if I wanted it to. But I reject the past
so I can have the pleasure of denying myself
as when I pass a row of flowers, acknowledging
their beauty (as they nod back, recognizing mine)
without crouching to cut them at the base
with my teeth or rip them from the ground,
gathering them to my chest like stolen gowns.
I leave the little beasts alone in their zoo of light
and turn to accept the admiration of the poor,
who nod and wonder at my enormous discipline,
which keeps them from killing and mounting me
on the walls of their otherwise tasteless, suburban homes.

With Cheerful Speed

We were spinning ourselves into a rare dessert,
a delicate sugar helmet, deliriously scribbled, snow
that would melt on contact with that other intractable world.
French King Henry took to wearing a basket of little dogs
on a ribbon around his neck. One famous architect
sat in the vespertine light in the lonely brilliance
of one recurring idea: that acid-stained titanium wing,
that corner he meant for more than his dream—
what is there now? A vase, dust, a precocious child?
There are many ways of swallowing death for the stone
that it is. My mother liked me to hang from the upstairs
banister and sing opera through the railings. Cranking
all the windows closed, con brio, then reaching
the end of the hall, wanting an endless hall with more
windows to shut before the storm—this was
my mother's version of transport.
Some of us are looking for a smoother transition,
the name of a loved one, a movie star.
The English called it *sprezzatura*, the ability to think
an impossible lightness into the body and leap over
a mess of tombs thereby escaping your godbound
enemies or by the flourishes of a sword
cut the gown into a hundred bits leaving the woman
that had been so tightly bandaged in tulle more or less
naked not even nicked by the sword.
What woman suddenly stripped to a breeze

she had only felt on her hands and face
would not make that premarital leap? She is
the lucky beneficiary of another's studied
effortlessness. You will carry her across death
because you have matched yourself
to nothingness and she has not.

PROSPECTS

One daughter more lovely than the last.
Each a burning threshold, so fearless, so hygienic.
One shaking her fringe and breaking bones doing it,
another strapping herself to a prow for luck.
Each daughter more grammatical, more game.
But you should have seen how they treated their mother,
who only lived to love them, to offer them fruit
in storms she had conjured. To let them swim in public
fountains and jump ravines in heavy skirts.
How they hauled her about in silences. Or ripped her
in two with refusals. How they seized her and shook her
and blasted her with insults (You zero! You peasant!)
while she remained unmoved, unhurt, her joy inviolable.
They kept kicking her shins under the table
and biting her ankles when she tried to walk away
as if they didn't quite get what a mother was. Didn't they
have a dictionary? Weren't they tall and grammatical?
Under *mother* it reads: bright blinding void.
How stupid they looked trying to take apart a void.
Once they were young, so tall they teethed on the moon.
But now they were all grown up. They were full
of narrow staircases and dark landings
on which I once wanted to meet them.

Winding Sheet

The suitors are doing donuts in the parking lot.
Another playing chess, another baking
me a hive choked with marzipan bees. Erupt,

erupt, my mouth the other hive. I've set up
the games there because I'm game as much
as they: piñata, the prisoner's dilemma. . .

Who folds his breath tightest into his paper
football and flicks it into the stream gets
to take down the flag. Still in hysterics.

Bed it down in a drawer. Bed
of olive. Bed of oak. Bed of laughing at
the leaving, at the literal, the laugh.

Range your mind north, to where I am
night's prescription and its open sore. I eat.
I sleep. I eat the suitors' sleep and stitch

an obsolete stitch. But I would rather be
happy. Once, without dreaming, I woke up
with the taste of another woman.

Tell me, what's lotus? You'd say, lock
myself in, close the window and excavate
the heaven-prone articulate sky.

I am devout or with you watching.
Pig or god, I am learning how it's done.
I have never been a genius of anything but you.

Mare Clausum

One sure way of getting behind
God's back is by making a trumpet
of some devil's minion's ass in a poem
O mondo immondo! about the cosmo-
graphy of the universe, whose greater
author is God, Himself, as Dante does
in the Inferno, at the end of Canto XXI.
A simpler but no less sure way is to
spin off the curb in a fit of laughter
like dry leaves when you find me
sitting on your doorstep. As if I were
waiting to get in and drown in your
wardrobe. *Crudelis, crudele*, pricked
by a love you cannot return in kind.
So Beatrice became the crown of Dante's
moods all the while she spoke to him
and ground him down to a pilgrim
with her stare; you made me a means
in your bed. It was dark at the back
of the storefront, and the fan was a fetish,
its bucking and breeze. I bruised
easily and you scoured me in the stall,
as if I'd been walking for water, digging
and making forts for years, now that was all
over; I had to go to work. But there
was Matty getting sun against the brick

spilling out the stories like unstrung beads
on cement—boys who dove deep for
watermelon choked with five-dollar bills,
and who was it who crushed it on
the bottom with a tire iron and never came
up for air. Who? The sun barked us back.
Speluncam eandem Dido et dux
Trojanus deveniunt. I lost my job.
That night Mary from Philly tended bar.
Wise she was from letting us drink ourselves
to death. Pints-under I pretended I
knew her from row-house days in North-
east Philly, that she had been my baby-
sitter. Next day we found a pool. This time
the park unlocked, no membership
needed, kids dipping their heads into the
fountain and filling cups to pour onto
their mothers. Kids happy to run back
and empty, run back and fill. The pool had
been drained. That blue so medicinal, the black
lines lovely as animals as they followed the slant
toward the deep end and climbed the wall.
You said, I think I'll keep my clothes on, then
jumped in and swam the butterfly methodically.
By now there were boys racing up and down
the slope of the deep end. When the Queen

saw this, she thought, when I first met Raleigh,
I called him My Oracle, but then I
learned to call him Water. And she was not
a stuttering Queen. She was a virgin.
I never went home those days. I was home-free.
I called my machine to hear my sober voice.
That was earth, back in Brooklyn, where with no
one on watch, my Chinese orchid bloomed.

Cho-fu-Sa

How far exactly is Cho-fu-Sa? Will I ever know
the distance one can travel away from the self to another

without breaking apart, until I have arrived, white-hot
and thirsty, looking to tie one on in a three-syllable town:

the lover, the beloved, and the invisible wilderness between them
mottled with light. How will I know this port town is the right

town until I stand at its wall, ripened by the miles I've walked.
Never mind that love contracts the world, that if you bind

your breath together, we are only one breath away. Let us in.
We have fistfuls of seed, foreign coins, and gold string,

blossoms and wishes, buttons that fell from your cuff.
Those days you were tenaciously single, ecstatic with resolve

to hold out for the one, the town of two-in-one.
Where the swell rushes the shore nonchalantly, striking like a vow

until there's no more sand to strike upon. Let us in
to lob our small gifts. The arms fly out with abandon.

Hand to open. Hand to open. Hands opening as you pass.
If you should look back to find us scrambling behind you, sweeping

the floor for grain or confetti caught and freed by your veil,
who can blame us? No—embrace us, lock us into your town.

We won't be here much longer. Because this is the part when
you want to be alone, when you feed us to the tigers and kiss.

*** YEARS OLD

And still in this body knowing all I know
like how to bust a mirror with my head
the mirror where I practiced how to kill
and spare a life all in one look how many
looks I have built and destroyed for love
until I faced the sunset prostitution
in my burning chaps. Against me something
became something else. Upon me orchids
into assassins daily. An eyelash on a lip
about to speak became an ember a vulture
that flew off and rode the valley for fun.
So much blonde surrender in the brush
and in the surf while a brunette childhood
steamed on ice. The blue was so available
then as it still is now where I clean up my
mess and hold a piece of mirror to the sun.
In these small ways I start a couple fires.

CODA

Apart from the world I wish to thank
the waves that held me back from you.
Finders, says the sea, it thinks it's still
a child. Keepers, says the sea, as if it could.

NOTES

p. 9   The title borrows a fragment from Heraclitus.

p. 22   *Skaz* is a Russian word derived from the word "skazat,"
to tell. It refers to oral, improvised speech.

p. 28   "The Headdress" borrows from *Hamlet*. In Act II, scene ii,
Hamlet says, "...there is nothing either good or bad, but thinking
makes it so."

p. 43   The title of the poem is stolen from a line in *The Wasteland*,
by T.S. Eliot.

p. 56   A "Mare Clausum" is an enclosed sea. "Speluncam eandem
Dido et dux Trojanus deveniunt": Dido and the Trojan leader
went down into that self-same cave. From *The Aeneid*.

p. 59   "Cho-fu-Sa" refers to Ezra Pound's "The River-Merchant's
Wife: A Letter." In her letter, the wife writes that she will come as
far "Cho-fu-Sa" to meet her husband.

Also Available from saturnalia books:

The Girls of Peculiar by Catherine Pierce

Ladies & Gentlemen by Michael Robins

Xing by Debora Kuan

Other Romes by Derek Mong

Faulkner's Rosary by Sarah Vap

Gurlesque: the new grrly, grotesque, burlesque poetics
edited by Lara Glenum and Arielle Greenberg

Tsim Tsum by Sabrina Orah Mark

Hush Sessions by Kristi Maxwell

Days of Unwilling by Cal Bedient

Letters to Poets: Conversations about Poetics, Politics, and Community
edited by Jennifer Firestone and Dana Teen Lomax

The Little Office of the Immaculate Conception by Martha Silano
Winner of the Saturnalia Books Poetry Prize 2010

Personification by Margaret Ronda
Winner of the Saturnalia Books Poetry Prize 2009

To the Bone by Sebastian Agudelo
Winner of the Saturnalia Books Poetry Prize 2008

Famous Last Words by Catherine Pierce
Winner of the Saturnalia Books Poetry Prize 2007

Dummy Fire by Sarah Vap
Winner of the Saturnalia Books Poetry Prize 2006

Correspondence by Kathleen Graber
Winner of the Saturnalia Books Poetry Prize 2005

The Babies by Sabrina Orah Mark
Winner of the Saturnalia Books Poetry Prize 2004

Velleity's Shade by Star Black / Artwork by Bill Knott

Polytheogamy by Timothy Liu / Artwork by Greg Drasler

Midnights by Jane Miller / Artwork by Beverly Pepper

Stigmata Errata Etcetera by Bill Knott / Artwork by Star Black

Ing Grish by John Yau / Artwork by Thomas Nozkowski

Blackboards by Tomaz Salamun / Artwork by Metka Krasovec

My Scarlet Ways was printed using the font Palatino.

www.saturnaliabooks.org